The  ary

Real Meanings

HORATIO NETHERWALLOP

ORGANIST PUBLICATIONS

© Organist Publications 2007
The Organist's Dictionary of Real Meanings

ISBN : 978-0-9550749-1-2
Published by Saucepan Lid Publishing
distributed by Organist Publications Ltd
PO Box 538
Epsom
Surrey
KT19 9EY

A CIP catalogue record of this book
can be obtained from the British Library.

Book designed by Michael Walsh

Printed by
RPM Print & Design
2-3 Spur Road
Chichester
West Sussex PO19 8PR

Cover cartoon by Hilary Perona-Wright

ABOUT THE AUTHOR

Horatio Netherwallop wanted to serve the Church in an important leadership role but, finding that he could not master the organ, he became a clergyman instead.

However his musical career was not abandoned. He soon mastered the electric kettle as a pupil of the Mopp-Handel School of Domestic Studies. His mastery of domestic refreshment procurement strategy was quickly acknowledged when he was awarded a Nectar Points certificate by Sainsbury's, one of the country's largest suppliers of coffee.

His postgraduate studies allowed him to travel overseas to study the "infusion method" with Dr Kofi Pot. He further acquired the skill of blending orange-based drinks with water and thus gained a new younger following.

His skills with the kettle were demonstrated at the world premier of Ivan Heddake's *Symphonic Migraine for Massed Orchestra and Bass Telephone* in 1974 when he entertained the entire audience during the interval, both of whom praised his creativity. The following year he undertook a world tour of Tooting Broadway.

He is much in demand as a freelance session coffee-maker by many of the world's leading musicians. Although modern coffee machines can be programmed to provide a fairly convincing coffee, he still believes that they cannot equal the quality of the professionally qualified and experienced *café produceur.*

In 1992, he was appointed as the country's first full-time Diocesan Adviser on Coffee. He quickly established excellent relations with the coffee companies and supermarkets, and started collaborative ventures with other churches. He has produced diocesan guidance on coffee and is available to give talks to church groups. His bishop has praised his enthusiasm in "this ground-breaking exciting new ministry".

In 2004, he was invited to discuss coffee with some church musicians but, finding only guitarists present, he went to the church office and wrote this book. He was recently rediscovered filed under K for Rubbish, having befriended a paper clip.

The work faithfully explains the real meanings of many terms which the church organist is likely to discover in the course of his or her work, omitting only terms which the organist will never encounter, such as "that was very good, would you like a pay rise?"

DICTIONARY

A 440   Standard of musical pitch, named after a road in Worcester.

A cappella   Music which the choirmaster is determined will be sung unaccompanied. He maintains this uncompromising position right until the final run-through.

A due   Involving two people, such as when the organist has not been paid the due fee for a wedding three weeks ago.

A flat major   What you get when a grand piano has fallen off the top of a roof at Sandhurst.

A flat minor   What you get when a grand piano falls down a mine shaft.

A tempo   Indication to a choir to sing at any speed they like.

ABA   Representation of ternary form where the first statement is repeated after the second. In the 1970s a new variant appeared known as ABBA.

Abundance   Blessing sought by churches, usually with a caller, live band and fish-and-chips supper — "and it's jolly good fun".

Accelerando   Instruction for a choir not to slow down.

Accent   Indication of where the strong beat of a word or phrase should be. A London accent indicates where a beat may go; a Liverpool accent indicates that the beat better go there; and a Scottish accent indicates that "there'll be trouble if it doesn't go there Jimmy".

Acciaccatura   Term which means a crushed note. The word is believed to come from the sound of putting a guitar through a mangle.

Accidental   Wrong note.

Accolade   Sign linking two or more staves. Church organists encounter this extensively in their music, which is just as well as they won't encounter it anywhere else.

Accompaniment   (1) A keyboard player to a choir
(2) A desperate soprano soloist to a conductor

Accordion   Instrument which looks like a radiator, works like a filing box, feels like a cushion and has similar musical properties to all three.

Acetone	Good sound. At least that is what you tell the music group leader when you invite him to inhale it.
Acoustic	Used to play snooker.
Act	Performance which involves dramatic skills as well as musical ones. Acts are divisions of an opera and what the organist does when the worship committee wish to share some ideas.
Acting career	Full-time unemployment.
Action	(1) Part of a piano mechanism. (2) Part of choir mechanism when choral evensong is cut.
Action song	Song with movements, such as when the choir walks out.
Acute	Sharp and shrill, as in "I heard a cute soprano".
Ad hoc	Polite term for style of music played by church music groups.
Ad lib	What a composer writes on the score when he cannot be bothered to write proper music.
Ad libitum	A premiere.

Adagio

Slow. An indication of the speed at which congregations sing hymns, as opposed to andante (slow), moderato (slow), allegro (slow) and presto (slow).

Added sixth

What the choir does when told that it is disgraceful to drink five pints after a choir practice.

Address

Poorly prepared sermon.

Adolescence

The age between puberty and adultery.

Advent

Part of the church year for holding school carol services.

Air

A tune or melody. It is favoured by organists but not by music group leaders. Organists agree that music group leaders should not have access to air.

Al

Italian for "to", as in *al fine* = to the end, *al Coda* = to the Coda, *al martino* = two Spanish eyes.

Aleatoric

Type of music where some element of the performance depends on chance, such as whether the tenors turn up.

All Things Bright and Beautiful

Hymn by Mrs Alexander which

loses one verse about every thirty years. Around 1950 we stopped believing that God made the rich man in his castle and the poor man at his gate. Around 1980 we stopped believing that God made the reeds we gather every day. It is predicted that by 2040 we will have stopped believing that God made little birds and flowers.

Allegro

Fast. The term is believed to be a corruption of *all aggro* describing a choir practice.

Altered chords

In proper music, a term sometimes used to describe chromatic modulation. In church music group parlance, it describes an organist in frivolous mood.

Alto

Female singer who can read music.

Alto clef

Ancient clef no longer used for musical instruments but still used for violas.

Ambrosian chant

Style of singing used for advertisements for creamed rice.

Amen

Expression which affirms a belief in prayer. It is often said when some tenors and basses make a guest appearance at choir practice.

America　　　　　　　One nation under God, liberty, and
　　　　　　　　　　　　burger and chips with a large diet Coke.

American organ　　　Instrument like a harmonium except
　　　　　　　　　　　　that it sucks.

American organist　Twice the price; half the quality.

Ancient and Modern A hymn book of ancient and even
　　　　　　　　　　　　more ancient hymns.

And also with you　One of the responses said or
　　　　　　　　　　　　sung after the minister has said
　　　　　　　　　　　　something, such as "there seems
　　　　　　　　　　　　to be something wrong with this
　　　　　　　　　　　　microphone".

Andantino　　　　　　Diminutive form of "andante"
　　　　　　　　　　　　which means "slow". So
　　　　　　　　　　　　"andantino" means either more
　　　　　　　　　　　　slow or less slow, making it one of
　　　　　　　　　　　　the least useful musical terms.

André Previn　　　　Conductor who achieved great
　　　　　　　　　　　　success after appearing on
　　　　　　　　　　　　Morecambe and Wise Show.

Anglaise　　　　　　A country dance which is clearly
　　　　　　　　　　　　English in nature — hence the use
　　　　　　　　　　　　of a French term.

Announcements　　　The point in the service where the
　　　　　　　　　　　　vicar says something like "How
　　　　　　　　　　　　beauteous are their feet who stand
　　　　　　　　　　　　by Charles Villiers Stanford".

Answer	Second theme in a fugue. The word has other meanings but a church organist is not likely to encounter them.
Anthem	Part of the service where the choir reminds the congregation that they haven't been disbanded yet.
Anticipation	The normal excuse for coming in on the wrong note.
Antiphon	One of a two-part arrangement. The other part is known as a Deciphon.
Antiphony	Where one part of the choir answers back to what has been said. The term only relates to performance. In rehearsal this practice is known as misbehaviour.
Antonyms	Words which have opposite meanings, such as "musician" and "church music group member".
Apologetics	When theologians explain why they do not accept that they are wrong.
Applause	Tepid clapping enthusiastically led by the performer's wife and children.
Appoggiatura	Indication that a composer meant to write a quaver instead of a crotchet.

Appreciation   The high regard in which an organist is held after he has left a church.

Archbishop of Canterbury
Someone who personifies the unity of the hopelessly divided Anglican Church. Recent occupants of the office have done remarkably well despite the small difficulty that the job is completely impossible.

Archives   Where Noah kept his bees.

Arco   Instruction in music for a string player to use a bow, or designatory letters which allow an organist to take a bow.

ARCO   Absolute Rubbish Church Organist.

Aria   Area taken by a sopreeno soloist.

Armonica   (1) Another name for the glass harmonica.
(2) Harmonica from the East End of London.

Ars antiqua   Polite name for an old bum.

Arsis   A weak beat, which must not be disjointed. Hence the expression, "he doesn't know his arsis from his elbow".

Art of Fugue   Something Bach started writing to try to prove to us that there is such a thing. He died in the attempt.

Arts Council   Body which requires musical bodies to complete many forms to find out why they won't get any public money.

As moll   (1) German term for A flat minor
(2) English term for curate's wife

Associated Board   Examining body in music. The organ is examined from grades 4 to 8. Each grade requires a higher level of performing skill from the student, for example:
Grade 4: moaning about the vicar
Grade 5: playing too loudly
Grade 6: drowning the choir
Grade 7: hating the music group
Grade 8: becoming immune to criticism

At the Boar's Head   (1) Opera by Holst.
(2) Research for the same regularly undertaken by choir.

Atonality   Lack of tone favoured by some modern composers and all church music groups.

Attacca   Musical term meaning "attack". Used to indicate a prompt start to a later movement, such as any attempt to disband the choir.

Audience Group of people who attend concert halls to cough, sneeze, drop programmes, rustle sweet packets, receive calls on mobile phones and tell their neighbour that their hearing aid has packed up.

Audition The act of putting oneself under extreme duress to satisfy the sadistic intentions of someone who has already made up his mind.

Augmented Harmony where the dominant is sharpened, or a choir with tenors.

Aulos Early Greek double-reed instrument. It is related to the music group clarinet known as the "ded-los".

Avant-garde Modern form of music which is usually also avant-tune, avant-harmony, avant-rhythm and avant-any-audience.

Ave Maria What a cockney said to his mate who wondered which girl he should marry.

B flat Unnecessary instruction to the altos.

B Mus Bad Musician

Babysitting Young people pretending to be grown-ups while grown-ups pretend to be young people.

Bach

German composer (1685-1750) who wrote music for examinations in organ playing.

Bach chorale

Where cowboys keep their hosses.

Bach family

Family of many musicians of whom JS Bach is the most famous. Other members include BARE Bach who wrote riding tunes, CALL Bach who wrote ring tones, OUT Bach who wrote Australian music, and GET Bach who wrote for The Beatles.

Bagpipes

Music instrument comprising a chanter and drone pipes. Its main attraction is that it sounds just the same when a person has learned how to play it as when they started.

Balaam's donkey

Creature through which God spoke (Exodus 22:28). Ever since, preachers have striven to be the mouthpiece of God and thus attain the spiritual status of a donkey.

Balanced

An organ swell pedal usually is, which is more than can be said for most organists.

Balls

Lavish dances which provide occasions of fine music and great company. Organists often refer to them when listening to suggestions from worship committees.

Band	Term used for church music group. Organists often express the view that "they should be band".
Bar	A natural division of music, so called because that is where the choir feels at home.
Bar line	Brass section during the interval.
Baritone	The usual excuse for not being able to sing the tenor part properly.
Baroque	Financial status of a tarumpeter.
Barrel organ	The two things which make an organist's life complete.
Bass	Person who sings at the bottom. (It often sounds like it.)
Bass clef	What you bump into if not looking where you are going on the seafront.
Bass drum	Instrument which provides a dull thud, but then who has ever heard an interesting thud?
Bass guitarist	Double insult.
Basse chantate	Bass with a voice suitable for melodic delivery and lyrical parts. They are most commonly seen flying on pigs when the moon is blue.

Bassoon What a fisherman hopes to catch.

Baton Means of conveying instructions, particularly to a cricket team.

Beat How you get a viola to keep the tempo. The downbeat is on the head, and the upbeat is on the chin.

Beats in the bar Good reason to try the next pub down the road.

Bee's wedding Mendelssohn's *Song Without Words* op 67 no 4. The organist has still not been paid.

Bell A large hollow device with an empty head, which has a long tongue and makes a loud repetitious noise. It differs from a music group leader in being made from metal.

Bells Means by which tone colour is added to music. It can be taken with water or ginger ale.

Berlioz French composer (1803-1869). His mother was a devout Christian and his father a devout atheist. He satisfied them both by writing much beautiful church music but not believing it.

Bigamy Only crime where two rites make a wrong.

Birth control   Prevention of pregnancy. Methods include the pill, condoms and dating church music group members.

Biscuits   Stale pieces of hard tack on the plate with the coffee. In fact, most churches do provide some chocolate biscuits, but the children scoff them all before the organist can get one.

Bishop   (1) Chess piece that cannot move in a straight line but always goes off at an angle.
(2) Senior clergyman named for a similar reason.

Bishop's robes   Bishops traditionally wear purple shirts and bright vestments. This is necessary as they are generally such grey characters they would not otherwise be seen in front of the stonework.

Blue   (1) Disgusting, filthy and pornographic.
(2) Sharing the values of the Conservative party

Blues   Any song played slowly which starts "woke up this morning".

Bold experiment   Vicar's idea that went wrong.

Bore   (1) Internal width of a wind instrument which determines its tone.

14

(2) Tone of a preacher which determines that his internal width is full of wind.

Bossa nova

Latin dance rhythm, named after the sound produced by a foreman's car.

Bottom line

Part of the music where all the bum notes are.

Brass

(1) Family of instruments including the trumpet.
(2) Colloquial term for money their players never have.

Brawl

An old country dance. Often performed at church gatherings.

Breathing

Natural function of the body. Much performance of church music can be improved by controlling the breathing. Choirs should breathe in the right places and music groups should stop breathing completely.

Bridge

(1) Part of a guitar from which the strings are suspended.
(2) Part of a highway from which the guitarist should be suspended.

Broadband

All female group.

Broken chords

Arpeggios, or mis-spelling of an improved guitar.

Bull

(1) Statement which is such rubbish that it is considered to have the value of cow dung.
(2) An authoritative statement from the Pope.

Buxtehude

Danish composer (1637-1707) who wrote fine organ music and wanted Bach to marry his daughter. He inspired Bach to write organ music and marry someone else.

Byrd

English composer (1543-1623) who wrote music in many styles. His sombre music is known as Black Byrd; his music with flattened sevenths is known as Blue Byrd; his highly ornamented music is known as Dolly Byrd; and pieces of doubtful authenticity are known as Dicky Byrd.

C flat

What a music group leader does before he decides he cannot afford to move out of his parents' home.

C sharp

Key used by composers on a really bad day.

Cacophony

Music group rehearsal.

Cadence

The part when everybody hopes you're going to stop.

Cage

(1) American composer of experimental music.

(2) Where he should be kept.

Cancan What a music group leader says when asked if he can strum two simple chords.

Candlemas What is left on the church carpet after a festival celebrated in February.

Canon (1) Obsolete offensive smooth bore which comes out with lots of old balls.
(2) An appropriate honour for a clergyman.

Canon law The rule which states that the photocopier breaks down just before printing the last page of the choir anthem.

Cantate domino Singing and playing games down the pub.

Cantus fermus Part given to someone who can only play four notes.

Capo Clip-device put round the neck of a guitar to hide the fact that the guitarist cannot play the chords as written. This needs to be distinguished from a device put round the neck of the guitarist which is known as "organist's hand".

Carol   Someone who turns up every Christmas.

Castanet   What a Spanish fisherman does.

Castor and Pollux   (1) Opera by Rameau.
(2) Term relating to moving a piano. The first term is how the piano should move; the second expresses the feeling when it does not.

Castrato   Man who sings without organ accompaniment.

Catechism   Bible study for pets.

Catechumenate   Cats home.

Catgut   Material for strings, so called because it comes from sheep.

CD-ROM   Computer Device Rendered Obsolete in Months.

Cello   How someone with a cold answers the phone.

Celtic worship   Service where meaningless text is relieved by meaningless music. In reality we know little about Celtic worship except that it died without trace long ago. Attending one of these services will tell you why.

Censer

Device to spread incense or moderate the choir's jokes.

Certitude

Basis for knowing the truth. It is the means by which clergy can be certain about Britain's foreign policy and defence commitments, though not so sure about the Virgin Birth and resurrection of Jesus.

Cha cha

Two Latin American tea dances.

Chanson de geste

How you describe a rugby song on a concert programme.

Chants

Music designed to allow the singing of prose, such as in the psalms. These are now rarely used, hence the expression "the chants would be a fine thing".

Chasuble

Part of a clergyman's dress. In the East End of London it is often worn with a Daveuble.

Children

Young people the church is desperate to attract so that they can not know what to do with them. Whatever children do — whether crayon scribblings or mumbled prayers — is praised to the skies. Under canon law, children may only be criticised if they sing in a choir.

Choir	Collective noun for all the opinionated nuisances found in a church congregation.
Choir practice	Occasion when choir members meet to exchange church gossip, moan about the vicar and agree that they have no time to rehearse any anthems.
Chopsticks	One of two things an organist can do with just two fingers. The other is making constructive criticism to the music group.
Chorale Fantasy	The tenors attend choir practice.
Chorus	"Bore us" transposed into an easier key.
Christening	Baptism of an atheist's baby.
Christingle	An orange with sweets, a candle and other things stuck on, each of which symbolises something. No-one has ever found out what, as the children are more interested in pinching the sweets, and the adults are more interested in calming down children who have burned their fingers while trying to pinch the sweets.
Christmas	The time of the year for the vicar's sermon against the world getting too commercial. Previously it celebrated the birth of Jesus Christ.

Churches Together A body which vainly tries to get Baptists and Roman Catholics to talk to each other; to get the Free Presbyterians to talk to anyone, and to get Anglicans to talk to other Anglicans.

Churchyard Grounds round a church. They often have many fine plants as the ground is often fertile, particularly if the church has no toilet.

Cinquième Obsolete name for viola. Unfortunately it is only the name which is obsolete.

Cipher A note which stays on after its key has been released. The organist has a choice of either removing the pipe or playing Messiaen.

Circular canon (1) Canon whose tune can be played endlessly.
(2) Canon whose fridge can be emptied endlessly.

Clavicytherium Crazy instrument; crazy name.

Clef Something which needs changing just before a solo from violas or tenors.

Clergy Those who wish to serve the church but are not clever enough to play the organ.

Clergy conferences A particular hazard for organists, as the vicar will come back with ideas about "some lovely music I heard while away" and which he wants to introduce. You can be sure it won't be Stanford in B flat, but a touchy-feely nursery rhyme for services where you hold hands and light candles. The best defence is for an organist to say he would love to introduce the music when he is properly trained after attending a course in four months time that costs £500. With four months to lose interest and the treasurer on your side, the suggestion should soon be forgotten.

Clerk in Holy Orders (1) In 16th century, a person who can write with a pen, and is therefore respected as the most literate man in the parish. (2) In 21st century, a person who can write with a pen, and is therefore disrespected as the most computer-illiterate man in the parish.

Clock Mechanical device which once told the time but now simply provides clanging noises at inappropriate moments.

Coates Several composers have this name. Albert (1882-1953) wrote operas, and is known as Top Coates. Eric (1886-1957) wrote light music and is known as Under Coates.

Cobblers

Shoe-menders. They are noted for their skill and quiet dedication, which is why organists often refer to them when discussing music with lay readers.

Coffee

A person who is coughed over.

Coffee time

Opportunity to chat with friends while three old ladies look blankly at an urn and wonder where they put the milk.

Col

With. This is usually used as an instruction to string players on how to attack their instruments. Useful terms are *col legno* (with the back of the bow), *col sega a catena* (with a chainsaw) and *col travolgere* (with a steamroller).

Collect

(1) A short prayer for the day said by the minister.
(2) A short job at the pub done by the music group leader.

Collection plate

Gong-sized dish of brightly coloured metal which has the unique property of becoming invisible in church entrances.

Coloratura soprano A singer who has great trouble finding the proper note, but who has a wild time hunting for it.

Commissioned work Any music which only ever receives one performance.

Committee Body established to find unworkable solutions to insoluble problems and thus to maintain the status quo. In most churches, the only committee which functions properly is the organist committee — with a membership of one.

Common metre What the conductor wants when he sees an attractive soprano.

Common time (1) Music in the 4/4 tempo.
(2) Time an organist spends talking with the congregation.

Compound time Opportunity for an organist to exercise out of his cell.

Computers Machine which can produce programmes and posters, index libraries, send messages and typeset music. If a problem arises with a computer, the organist should either seek the services of an expensive consultant or ask the youngest choirboy.

Con Musical term meaning "with", as in *big con* meaning a talk with the vicar about an organist's terms of engagement.

Concerto Musical contest between a player and an orchestra.

Concertina Organists' car after he drove while listening to Widor.

Conductor Someone who waves his arms around in an attempt to discourage performers.

Conference Process of multiplying the confusion of one man by the number of people present.

Confidential Instruction that the information must be broadcast round the parish as a matter of urgency. If you want something not to be generally known you put it on the notice board.

Console Musical term for either the part of the organ where the player sits or what someone else must do to the organist when the hymn list includes *If I Were a Butterfly*.

Consonant Letter sound which is not a vowel. Clear consonants are essential for the audience to understand what is being sung. Correct consonants are therefore more important than open bowel sounds.

Constructive criticism The usual excuse for being rude about the music.

Contract To reduce. So called because the document given to organists reduces in significance as the years go by.

Contralto A word which now means altos, particularly female ones. It literally means "against altos", but this meaning is now conveyed by the term "everyone".

Contrary motion Choir processing out as the music group walks in.

Conventions Respecting the traditions of different churches. For example, if holding an ecumenical service at 3pm, you ask the American Episcopalians to attend at 1500 hours, you ask the Anglicans to attend at three o'clock in the afternoon, and you ask the Irish Free Church to attend when the big hand is on 12 and the little hand on 3.

Cor Horn. For some reason this instrument is often suggested to any passing attractive young lady.

Cor anglais French for "English horn". This refers to an instrument which is neither English nor a horn, but a form of oboe. The instrument is actually French but cannot be called a French horn because that term is used to describe another instrument — which is German.

Cornamuse   Organ stop or someone who finds this dictionary funny.

Cornet   Brass instrument suitable for dance bands and for holding ice cream.

Corno   (1) Italian term for a horn.
(2) English term when someone has trodden on your foot.

Cornopean   Stop on an organ where the church could not afford a trumpet.

Cosi fan tutte   Opera by Mozart about someone cooling down their feet on a hot day.

Cough   Something a member of the audience is required to do just as the music becomes quiet and delicate.

Counter tenor   This is easy as there is usually only one of them.

Counterpoint   Where you pay for your goods in a shop.

Couple

To connect two parts of the organ together, or two members of the choir who have done something similar.

Covent Garden

Place which affords much work to professional musicians, such as stacking banana crates, driving lorries, moving sacks of potatoes etc.

Cowbell

Instrument used by drummers to tell band leaders where they are.

CRB check

Checking that the organist does not have a criminal record. Fortunately murdering Bach and drowning the choir do not count.

Crescendo

Reminder to a performer that they been performing too loudly.

Criminal record

A CD of Celtic worship songs, or something else whose possession makes a person unsuitable to work with children.

Critic

Someone who reviews a performance. This involves checking that the performance did actually take place after the review was written.

Crook

(1) Part of a horn — either a piece of bent tubing or the person playing it.

(2) Something which accompanies a bishop, such as an archdeacon.

Cross fingering Used by woodwind players who are frustrated at not being able to play the right notes.

Crowd Welsh stringed instrument, or two people listening to one.

Crotchet Similar to knitting, but usually faster.

Cui Russian composer (1855-1918) who wrote a famous call.

Custom In church parlance, this is something done once before, as in "it is our custom". If done two years running, it is a "tradition", and after three years, it is a "long-standing tradition".

Cut common Description of 2/2 time used by those who have not heard the term "alla breve".

Cut time When everyone else is playing twice as fast as you.

Cycle (1) Collection of many works on one theme.
(2) Method of transport for those who perform them.

D C	Abbreviation which can mean da capo, dust cart, dead chicken, dopey cellist, dry cider or deafening crash. In music, it usually means the first, but don't bet on it.
D Mus	Dead Musician
D S al Coda	Direction for musicians to lose their place.
Dead pigeon	Traditional method of producing a stopped tone from organ pipes.
Dear friend	Description used by one church member when speaking to a fellow member he is about to insult. If he begins "my dear beloved brother in Christ", find yourself a libel lawyer.
Deep	Another word for "thick".
Deep meaning	A worship song which has more than ten words.
Descant	A chance for sopranos to show that it is not just the tune they can get painfully wrong.
Designatory letters	Letters after someone's name indicating the music degrees and diplomas they have. Such musicians cannot play any better, but they can better explain why they play so badly.

Detaché	Instruction that trombones should play with the slides removed.
Di lasso	In the style of Italian cowboys.
Diatonic	A low-calorie drink by Schweppes.
Dictionary	One should be kept in the church, as it is the only way that appreciation comes after anthem.
Diminished chord	How to confuse a guitarist (along with major sevenths, suspended fourths and thirteenth chords).
Diminished triads	Hong Kong gangs after a police operation.
Diminuendo	Instruction for choirs suddenly to reduce the volume.
Diplomacy	The art of telling someone to go to Hell so nicely that they look forward to the journey.
Director of music	Church organist on an ego trip.
Discord	What was played instead of dat cord.
Dissent	State which occurs in the church when the choir is protesting and the music group is revolting.

Divine guidance The belief that:
- (a) God is bothered what hymns are sung at St Blogg's on Sunday,
- (b) God chose not to share this wisdom with those who choose the hymns;
- (c) inexplicably God shared this only with the speaker, and
- (d) by an amazing coincidence they just happen to be the speaker's favourites.

Divisi Indication that the composer cannot work out which note should be sung by a particular voice.

Do-re-mi Basis of all music, namely that dough will bring sunshine when paid to me.

Dogma A bitch of a teaching.

Doh What the alto is trying to find. What the organist is also trying to find, though for a different reason.

Dolce Musical term meaning "soft and sweet". Often applied to music; rarely applied to organists.

Dominant Relationship of the fifth note to the tonic, or of a soprano soloist to the conductor.

Doppelschlag German term for the musical ornament called a "turn" but which makes it sound a whole lot more exciting.

Dorian Mode Old lady who wrote some nice tunes.

Dotted note Indication to musicians to get the rhythm wrong.

Double bassoon Very expensive instrument used to make the sound of a wet raspberry.

Double choir What you have when two tenors turn up.

Double flat Where two altos live or how they sing.

Double sharp Rare piece of musical notation used by composers who hate performers.

Down bow Movement used by violinists when the rehearsal overruns.

Driving bass Music where the bass guitar dictates the tempo. It is widely regarded as a serious road hazard.

Drummer Someone who likes being with musicians.

Dump (1) Doleful piece of music written in 17th and 18th centuries.
(2) Music rehearsal room.

Duple time

(1) Rhythm where alternate pulses are accented.
(2) What the organist thinks he should be paid when the bride is 20 minutes late for her wedding.

E flat

How a choirmaster from Somerset comments on a tenor solo.

Early music

When the parts you hired arrive before the final rehearsal.

Easter

Holiday season in Spring. Despite its being well publicised as a holiday time, many clergy still insist on having services.

Ecclesiastical modes

Structure for liturgy. In chanting they have names such as Lydian and Hypolydian. In preaching they have names such as Boring and Hypoboring.

Echo

Effect of sound repeating when bounced off a hard surface, like a stone wall or the music group leader's head.

Ecumenism

The view that different churches should work together. It is believed by everyone and practised by no-one.

Egalitarian

Description of the practice whereby organists graciously no longer require lay readers and curates to bow down to them.

Electricity

Source of power for organ blowers and amplifiers. Electricity can be lethal, so great care is needed. If there is doubt about whether a connection is live, this should be carefully tested by asking the music group leader to put his fingers on it.

En chamade

Horizontal, when applied to organ pipes. The equivalent French term for the organist is *intoxicé*.

Encore

Response demanding additional music at a concert. The performer carefully organises his friends to lead this spontaneous response.

Enharmonic

Giving the right note the wrong name.

Enigma variations

Gamine? Negima?

ENSA

World War II music organisation. Stands for *Every Night Something Awful*

Envelope

(1) The growth and decay of a sound in electronic music.
(2) The piece of stationery giving someone's opinion of electronic music.

Epistle

(1) One of the letters in the New Testament.
(2) According to a Scotsman, the person who wrote it.

Equal temperament

When everyone in the choir is completely bonkers.

Eroica

Work people only attended because they thought the letter T had broken on the typewriter.

Excellent musician

Vicar's description of an organist he is about to sack.

Execution

How a piece of music should be performed, and what should happen to a music group leader after he has performed it.

Exegesis

When a theologian gives a learned answer to a question that no-one has asked.

Experience

Collective noun for mistakes.

Exposition

Part of a fugue where the organist gets arrested.

Expression

(1) Indications as to how music should be performed.
(2) Look on the conductor's face when it is.

F

Musical term which means everything from "silent" to

"deafening" to choirs. It has a quite different meaning when the organist uses it about the music group.

F sharps What an organist says when looking at Messiaen's harmony.

Fair trade Practice of drinking expensive coffee which tastes like ditch water to salve churchgoers' consciences about starvation in the Third World.

Faith partners Members of other religions. The modern virtue of working with our faith partners was previously known as the sin of pluralism.

Fall A cadence, particularly one which an organist is anxious for the music group leader to learn.

False relation Someone wanting to claim an inheritance.

Falsetto Tenor who is not as good at jumping over fences as he thought.

Family service The usual penance for naughty organists.

Fantasia Piece played by an organist when he wants to show off. The term has faded from use in recent years as it is now realised that all organists want to show off.

Fantasy A composition depicting some wonderful capricious event, such as the choir following the conductor or the organist getting a pay rise.

Feedback Noise from improper use of an amplification system. Its sound is painfully annoying. The term is also used for congregational comments on music.

Fees Notes most favoured by most musicians.

Feminine ending (1) Where music ends on an unaccented note.
(2) *[censored]*

Fiddle Popular name for either a violin or a musician's tax return.

Fifth Bottle of Jack Daniels. A diminished fifth is a half-empty bottle; a perfect fifth is a full bottle; an augmented fifth is two bottles; a hidden fifth is another bottle in the choir cupboard.

Figure (1) A pattern of melody or accompaniment.
(2) What a successful soprano soloist needs.

Figured bass Method of indicating harmony never used in performance. Its sole purpose is to prevent proper musicians passing examinations.

Filter   Device on modern recording equipment to cut out unnecessary noise. It must be switched off when recording modern worship songs.

Fine   Term used to encourage musicians at the end of a performance.

First inversion   (1) A chord whose bass note is the mediant.
(2) How to relieve a choirboy of his sweets.

Flat   Indication to musicians to play one semitone lower. This indication is not necessary for altos.

Flue   What the organist has and what he hopes the music group leader will get.

Flutter tonguing   Device used in flute playing or to secure soprano solos.

Folk music   Simple songs which must be performed by singing through the nose, with eyes closed, and wearing a long dress and sandals (even if male).

Folksong   Tune which a composer does not want to admit writing.

Font

Part of a church for drowning babies who wish to become operatic sopranos.

Foolish bridesmaids

Former name given to the parable in Matthew 25:1-13. It must now be known as "the parable of the cerebrally challenged bridespersons".

For prayer

The usual way that a church member introduces salacious gossip about another member.

Form

Presentation of musical ideas in a way useful to determine which horse is likely to win in the 3:30 at Sandown.

Forty-two

The answer to the meaning of life, according to *Hitchhiker's Guide to the Galaxy*. Unfortunately no-one can remember the question.

Frank discussion

How a church secretary describes a blazing row at a church council meeting. This is distinguished from "a full and frank discussion" which means a punch-up.

FRCO

Abbreviation for *Fairly Rubbish Church Organist.*

Fretless bass

Special type of bass guitar to make it easier for the player to get the wrong notes.

Frets	(1) Markings on a guitar neck to tell the player where to put his fingers. (2) What the guitarist does before he has to play them.
Fugue	Piece of organ music where the different parts come in one after the other. In choral music, this is known as a badly rehearsed anthem.
Führer	German term for the subject of a fugue or for an organist who plays one.
Full organ	Organ registration when the vicar is still audible during a hymn.
Fundament	(1) The root note in a chord. (2) What you kick when the singer cannot pitch it.
Fundamentalist	Clergyman who still believes in God.
Funeral	The point at which you first appreciate a person's fine qualities.
Furioso	Musical term indicating that music is to be played in the manner of an organist who has just been asked to play *If I Were a Butterfly*.
Furniture stop	(1) Mixture stop on the organ (2) Visit to DFS to buy a sofa and wine rack for the choir vestry.

Fuss

(1) German term for a foot, meaning the part of an organ pipe below the mouth.
(2) English term for a proposal to set up a music group.

Fux

Austrian composer (1660-1741) whose name should be pronounced to rhyme with "hooks", particularly if you want to keep your job.

G string

Lowest string on violin. It is capable of producing a range of tones from great excitement to calm contentment.

Gapped scale

Scale with parts missing, used by modern composers and those who pay organists.

Gay Gordons

Scottish ministers trained in the USA.

Geige

Device to measure radioactivity in German violins.

Gene Robinson

A recently discovered gay gene whose influence is now widespread in the USA and Canada. Its symptoms include causing great pain to the whole body, muddled thinking, and an inability to relate to others.

Gentleman

Someone who can play a trombone but does not.

Giga	Booking for an Italian musician.
Giuseppe Verdi	Composer of operas (1813-1901) who had the good sense to be born in Italy. Had he been born in England, his name would have been Joe Green, which does not have quite the same quality.
Glissando	A technique adopted by string players for difficult runs.
Glee	(1) A secular composition for two or three voices. (2) Being told that the music group leader is ill.
Glockenspiel	A musical instrument. A good music group leader may be able to explain how the player blows it.
God has given me	Expression used by some charismatics when they introduce a song and want you to believe that God wrote it. It is amazing that God who is all-powerful, all-knowing and all-creative should have such problems with the rudiments of music. God apparently uses many pseudonyms to collect his royalties from Thank You Music.
God has told me	Indication that someone is going to be awkward about getting their own way. This is usually followed by "I have prayed about it", which means

43

that the person will have a tantrum when he does not get his own way.

Golden number Part of an explanation in the front of The Prayer Book explaining how to calculate the date of Easter. It usually takes at least four sermons before most choristers understand it.

Good grace When an organist does not respond with abuse to comments from a church member but offers to waive the fee for playing the organ at their parents' wedding.

Good organist Organist at a person's previous church.

Grace note A note which leads to another, because that is what the composer intended or the performer pretended.

Grade one The equivalent of a doctorate in music for a music group leader.

Gradual Second hymn in a Communion service, so called because that is where the sopranos gradually start to wake up.

Gramophone One of two types of musical device which needs to be wound up to produce any music. The other is a music group leader.

Grand	(1) Instrument played by concert pianists. (2) How much they earn in a year.
Grave	(1) Musical term which indicates that a piece of music is to be performed very seriously. (2) Where you find the choir member who sang it joyfully.
Great	(1) Main manual on the organ. (2) Musical expression which indicates that the worship group leader is ill.
Great organ	What the congregation should say more often.
Ground bass	(1) A basic bass line in a piece of old music. (2) The remains of a choir man who tried to sing it.
Guitar	An ideal instrument for use by church musicians — especially when they can't find a cricket bat.
Guitar break	Good idea.
Guitar chords	Simple method for indicating harmony in popular music. It is an extremely sensible and useful form of notation which is widely used, and is therefore not taught in music colleges.

Halle	Orchestra which plays half the Hallelujah Chorus.
Hallelujah	The music group leader has broken his arm.
Hammer	Part of a piano mechanism which can profitably be used on a guitar.
Hammerklavier	In the style of Jerry Lee Lewis.
Harmonica	Posh mouth organ.
Harmonium	Pedal organ which has many stops, all of which sound the same.
Harmony	Something practised by organists and avoided by church councils.
Harp	Something which can add a gentle beauty to music, in preference to Fosters or Carlsberg.
Harpsichord	Instrument which Sir Thomas Beecham said sounded like two skeletons copulating on a tin roof.
Harpist	Someone who spends half the time tuning their instrument, and the other half playing an out-of-tune instrument.
Harvest festival	Time of the year when the vicar preaches on the need to conserve the world's resources, or whatever

other politically correct idea is currently in fashion. Historically, it was the occasion to thank God for providing our food.

Hautboy Self-opinionated oboe.

Headbanger (1) Person who listens to heavy rock music.
(2) Organist when the music group is around.

Hearing Jewellery worn by a hostentatious person from Chelsea.

Heating Expensive device to keep churches above a comfortable temperature in summer so that it is broken by winter.

Heavy metal (1) A type of rock music characterised by a thunderous beat and blaring guitar solos.
(2) The material which is ideal for hitting performers of the above.

Heckelphone Obscure double reed instrument invented for church meetings.

Heel Term variously used to describe part of a violin bow, method of playing organ pedals, or someone in a church music group.

Hell (1) German term for clear or bright.

(2) English term for somewhere which is.

Hemidemisemiquaver   A note which is one sixteenth of a crotchet but whose main claim to fame is that it starts with three different prefixes meaning "half".

Heritage   The concept that, just because previous generations filled the church with junk, the present generation must keep it like that to inflict on future generations.

High mass   Heavy object delicately balanced on door of vicar's vestry.

Highland fling   How to deal with bagpipes.

Hired music   Music which is falling to pieces and appears on a peculiar grey paper caused by having marks added in pencil and then erased so that the next hirer can write them in again.

Hocket   (1) Term used for musical style where the melody line is broken by rests.
(2) Term used by trumpeters for what they must do when the rent is due.

Holding note   (1) Note sustained in one part while other parts are moving.
(2) How a person attracts an organist's attention.

Holiness	State of organist's socks.
Home visit	When a priest visits a sick member of the church. For the congregation, this is done to provide spiritual comfort. For the organist, this is done to make sure he really is ill and not skiving off to a better paid job at another church.
Homophonic	Form of choral singing found in American Episcopal church.
Honorary canon	Consolation prize to a clergyman who is not going to become archdeacon.
Hood	Garment worn by yobs to show that they are tough, have no feelings for others and do not want to be identified. Organists sometimes also wear one.
Hook	A catchy phrase in popular music. There are many different types which can be employed for church music groups, particularly the left hook and right hook.
Horn	Ill wind that nobody blows good.
Horsemen	The four Horsemen of the Apocalypse described in Revelation 6:1-8. They are traditionally known as War, Famine, Pestilence, and

Death. Ronnie Corbett suggests that there was a fifth rider called Mishap, but he fell off his horse.

Hospitality Making people feel at home when you wish they *were* at home.

Humanist Society A non-prophet organisation.

Humor German term for "humour". This term is rarely used.

Hymn list Details of the music which should have been played at a service. A hymn list is either good (chosen by organist) or bad (chosen by clergy).

Hymns Parts of the service to allow things to happen, such as the children leaving, collection bag taken round, windows opened etc.

I feel it is right How an evangelical says "I want". This may be followed by "I have prayed about it" or "I feel the Holy Spirit is telling me..." These expressions mean "I want, and I will be awkward if I don't get my own way."

Idyll Piece of a pastoral or romantic nature. Not generally associated with organists.

If I were a butterfly A song which has made organists finally acknowledge that perhaps *Wide Wide as the Ocean* was not so bad, after all.

Imperfect cadence Two chords which lead to another violin cadenza.

Impetuoso Organist after the sermon has gone on for 15 minutes.

Impressionism Using wrong notes to convey a general idea.

Improvisation Busking by a qualified musician. The term comes from an irregular verb — I improvise, you extemporise, he busks, they make it up as they go along.

Incumbent The person in charge of an Anglican church. The word is believed to be a corrupt form of *encumbrance.*

Indeciso A church council on being asked to spend money on music.

Inflection Boring bits of plainsong — as compared to the very boring bits.

Informal worship Liturgical equivalent of a two-year-old's birthday party.

Inner parts (1) Guts, intestines and offal.
(2) Altos and tenors.

Innocente   Musical term describing organist suspected of improvising on an unsuitable melody.

Inquisition   When one Christian burned another at the stake for not properly showing the love of Christ to the world.

Installation   Process followed by a church when it gets a new vicar or a new boiler.

Intercessions   Time in service when a member of the congregation prays that God will bless their church and sort out everything on the news in the last week. It is an opportunity for the organist to finish the paperwork he started during the sermon.

Intermezzo   A light musical entertainment about a conductor getting to know a low-voiced soprano.

Interval   The time it takes to find the right note.

Intonation   Singing through your nose.

Invention   (1) A short piece in contrapuntal style.
(2) Reason given by organist for changing the last hymn.

Inversion   Means of getting the rest of the drink out of the bottle.

Inverted turn	Australian bird.
Irregular metre	What happens to the wife of an absent serviceman.
Irresoluto	Church council meeting after a discussion on funding music.
Isorhythmic	Term used to describe a performance of a madrigal by singers using different editions.
Italian sixth	Form of augmented chord or diet of someone who likes ice cream.
Jack	Piece of wood attached to the key on a harpsichord or clavichord. A bright sound comes from a happy jack; a slow sound from a lumber jack; a crisp sound from a cracker jack; and a contented sound from an i'm-all-right-jack.
Jam session	When jazz musicians meet either to play music or to share the pot of jam one of them has finally been able to afford.
Jamb	Small ledge on each side of an organ manual to keep sweet wrappers, blunt pencils and three-month old hymn lists.
Jamming	Something which happens when musicians get together, particularly to photocopy music.

Job (1) Character in Old Testament who was treated badly and complained loud and long to God about it.
(2) Employment as a church organist.

Jubilate (1) Setting of psalm 100.
(2) Orange juice with lots of milk.

Just Intonation Singing only through your nose.

Kalimba Type of lamellaphone. (What do you mean: you're none the wiser?)

Kappellmeistermusik Literally, this is German for "choirmaster music". It has come to mean music which is technically correct but lacking in any aesthetic merit. This proves that the whole world really does hate choirmasters, and we are not just being paranoid.

Kazoo Simple musical instrument based on the principle of tissue paper and a comb. It imitates the sound of reed stops on early electronic organs.

Kettledrum A mate's house where you can get a cup of coffee.

Key Either the pitch of the music or a device to lock the store-room containing the music group's instruments. The organist vainly hopes that the altos will find it and the music group leader will not.

Key change What is needed when the music group leader wants to have a go on the organ.

Key signature The written name on the organist's pay cheque.

Kit Name for a small violin which is very easy to carry. Although the instrument has now been obsolete for many years, young female players are still often told to remove it.

Knee stop Device operated by a player's knee. On a harmonium it opens a swell box; on a harpsichord it brings in the octave strings; and in the groin it stops the conductor getting friendly.

Knot The ornamental fretwork which adorns the sound hole on guitars. Organists frequently suggest that guitarists be like adornments in the church, hence the expression "get knotted".

Krebs (1) German composer (1690-1762), student of Bach.
(2) South African seafood.

Kulturbolschewismus Term used in Nazi Germany to denigrate the music of Schöenberg and Stravinsky. The term died out because no-one could work out how to pronounce it.

L'istesso　　Musical term which indicates that the music which follows is to be played exactly as the music before. This term is not needed for viola parts.

Lagrimoso　　Sadness at running out of lager.

Lalo　　(1) French composer (1823-1892)
(2) What the organist does when he realises that the vicar recognised the rugby songs used in the voluntary.

Lambeth Conference A meeting organised every ten years by the Archbishop of Canterbury so that it can be boycotted by bishops.

Lamentoso　　Music for which a violinist needs two handkerchiefs.

Largamente　　Animated discussion about music after five pints of Fosters.

Largo　　Italian lager.

Lasso　　Two consecutive notes of a descending scale.

Latin　　One of the languages God understands. Many pieces have Latin names, such as *Pater Noster* for "Our Father", *Agnus Dei* for "Lamb of God" and *brevissimae bracae femineae* for "hot pants".

Latin text

Latin is discouraged in choir anthems chosen by the organist as it is not understood by the people and creates an impression of irrelevance to church visitors.
Latin is encouraged in Taizé chants chosen by the vicar, as they connote timelessness and universality and thus create an impression of relevance to church visitors.

Lay

A song of a traditional and lyrical nature or what the people would rather be doing than singing such songs.

Lay clerk

Men who sing in cathedral choirs. Several reasons have been put forward for this term, most of which are not printable.

Lay reader

Person who cannot preach a proper sermon but does not let that stop them.

Lead guitar

The guitarist who plays the tune in a group. If the tune is played properly, the first word is pronounced to rhyme with "reed".

Leader

First of the first violinists who has a special relationship with the conductor, who often refers to the "beloved leader" though sometimes an initial is used for the first word.

Lectionary Book which states what the preacher should be talking about, and which therefore serves as a guide for choosing the music. It became obsolete when the RSCM started publishing *Sunday by Sunday*.

Legando (1) An expression mark indicating the execution of two smooth strokes.
(2) What the conductor would like to stroke and what she says when he does.

Leger line Where a musician's debts are recorded.

Leggiero Musical term for something which sounds like fun.

Lent (1) Penitential season just before Easter.
(2) What the organist arranged for the music group's instruments to be, which explains why he was penitential just before Easter.

Lesser Term used by an organist to describe either a minor key or the curate.

Lesson A bible reading in church. Choirmasters are particularly keen that choirboys should learn from them, as in the expression "I'll teach you a lesson".

Liaison A musical term which indicates a tie or binding, either in musical notation or in a musician's love life.

Liberal In the church, a person who believes we should tolerate all points of view and does not tolerate anyone who disagrees with this view.

Lié French term meaning slurred, or English term where an organist explains why his speech is.

Liebfraumilch Eighteenth century German composer of church music. At least that is what you tell the church treasurer when you hand him the bill. You also explain that Reisling and Medoc are Italian composers, and that Johnny Walker is the organ tuner.

Lied (1) German term for a type of song expressing deep emotion.
(2) What the soprano did when asked if she could sing one.

Light bulb Something which provides illumination and endless jokes in church. An exception is for the organ pedal board where a light bulb serves only to fill a dead electrical socket.

Lilt To sing in a merry style, as if drinking fizzy grapefruit juice.

Lip

(1) Flat surface round the mouth of an organ pipe.

(2) Opinion on organ playing which leads to a thick surface round the mouth of the curate.

Litany

Question asked by the churchwarden before a candlelight service. The greater litany is when someone agrees to light the candles; the lesser litany is when no-one can find the matches.

Liturgy

Text which is prepared for use in worship. Examples include "you may now kiss the bride" and "we hope you will join us for a cup of coffee after the service".

Living

Position which a clergyman believes God wants him or her to fulfil — provided the luxury vicarage is in good condition, the local schools are good, the husband or wife can find a job, and the church council is generous with expenses.

Living by faith

Scrounging.

Loco

Back in the right place after admiring a steam train.

LRAM

Likes Ruining All Music.

Lulu

Opera by Berg. He did not finish it,

because he wanted to see what she did after having a hit with *Shout!*

Lure	Primitive horn, and what a primitive man used it for.
Lute	Old stringed instrument fondly desired by organists.
Madrigals	Unaccompanied polyphonic songs. So named from the body movements of those who sing them.
Maestro	Musician who aspires to be an organist.
Magnificat	Cat that got the cream.
Major	Term expressing something which is greater in music and lesser in prime ministers.
Major scale	Effort needed to get to the organ loft.
Male soprano	Male singer with a bushy beard and ten children, who plays rugby and drinks ten pints of beer each day — just so you don't get the wrong idea.
Manica	Italian term for fingering, or an Italian who tries to do it.
Mano sinistra	Someone the mafia uses to collect fees.

Manual   Keyboard used by an organist; work
                      done by a music group leader.

Maracas   Instruments shaken by Latin-
                      American percussionists and
                      soprano soloists.

March   (1) Composition of a strong rhythm,
                      such as the *Wedding March* by
                      Mendelssohn.
                      (2) When an organist gets paid for
                      playing it in October.

Masochism   Shouting "encore" to the church
                      music group.

Masculine ending Musical term for what every
                      soprano soloist seeks.

Mass in B minor   Work by Bach, so-called because
                      most of it is in D major.

Match   (1) Something used to light candles.
                      (2) Two things which equate to each
                      other, such as the curate's brain and
                      the organist's foot.

Maultrommel   German name for a Jews harp,
                      literally "mouth drum". The
                      instrument is neither a harp nor a
                      drum and has nothing to do with
                      Jews. Still the bit about mouth is
                      right.

Mean temperament Choirmaster on a good day.

Meaningful	Meaningless.
Measure	Word used by Americans to mean a bar of music. The word "bar" is too short for Americans who favour the enlengthenment of pretentionalistic vocabularisation when conversationalising.
Mediant	(1) Note which comes between the tonic and dominant. (2) Person who comes between the vicar and organist.
Melodic minor scale	Something else which is studied solely to pass music exams.
Melody	Girl who does not date modern composers.
Men	Italian and feminist term meaning "less".
Meno mosso	Indication that the performer is getting too excited.
Messa di voce	Instruction to singers to get their part wrong. Not necessary on the alto part.
Messe	(1) French or German term for a mass. (2) English term for choir vestry after the Christmas party.

Messiah

Either Jesus Christ as Saviour or a work by Handel. These two meanings have been known to cause concern, such as when organists ask each other if they have any spare Messiahs.

Metre

Measure of rhythm. Common metre means 8, 6, 8 and 6 syllables; long metre means 8, 8, 8 and 8 syllables; and gas metre means too many syllables.

Metronome

Goblin that lives in London.

Meyerbeer

German lager.

Mezzo-soprano

Woman who can't sing either soprano or alto properly.

Midnight mass

The popular service held during the night of Christmas Eve for the sole purpose of singing the last verse of *O Come All Ye Faithful*.

Military

Hymns which have military allusions such as *Onward Christian Soldiers* are now frowned on for being biblical.

Military titles

Many church officers retain former military titles, such as Cdr Bloggs. This allows them to be bossed about by General Synod and take charge of Major Disasters.

Miniature score	Twenty glasses of liqueur.
Minimal music	What is desired at youth services.
Minister	Person who acts as compere for the choir's weekly performance.
Minor scales	Skin covering of baby fish.
Minor second	Two altos singing in unison.
Mints	Unit of length of a sermon. One mint is a concise sermon. Two mints is a considered sermon. Thereafter it is background waffle while you sort your music and mark the choir register.
Minutes	(1) Record of a church meeting. (2) How long it should have lasted.
Miracle	The tenors turn up *and* the vicar preaches a good sermon.
Mirliton	Posh name for a kazoo
Missionary	Someone who goes overseas to promote Christianity. This is a most worthwhile job and a good position for a young man.
Mixed voices	Choir comprising singers and non-singers.
Mixture	(1) Organ stop which adds brightness to tone.

(2) Choir which adds nothing to tone.
(3) Combination of gravel and cement to help cure (2).

Mode   Scale with the black notes left out.

Modern jazz   Occasion when musicians meet and see for how long they can all make meaningless noises from their instruments while drinking beer and keeping their eyes closed.

Modern music   Misnomer. The second word has always been wrong, and the former fortunately now is also.

Modern pop music Music in a style found in the pop charts about 30 years ago and which the minister therefore thinks is appropriate to attract today's kids into the church.

Modesty   Not accepting praise when first offered in the hope that it will be offered again.

Modulation   When a young person buys a sharp suit and snazzy tie, and puts Brylcreem in his hair.

Money   The ultimate form of musical inspiration.

Mono	Prefix which means one, and is used in various musical terms, such as *monodrama* = stage work for one performer, *monothematic* = work based on one theme, *monotonous* = sermon from one vicar.
Mood	(1) Relationship between Long and Breve in mensural notation. (2) Relationship between choirmaster and choir when they get it wrong.
Moralities	Forms of miracle play. Not commonly found in the church today.
Morning Has Broken	Hymn sung at weddings to indicate that the couple have not been to church since they were baptised. (The other hymns will be *All Things Bright and Beautiful, Amazing Grace, Jerusalem* and *Give Me Oil in My Lamp.*)
Morris dance	Old form of English dance from 15th century which involves men dressing up in white, and prancing around with bells round their ankles and banging sticks. Because it is so ancient, everyone is too polite to say how daft it is.
Mouth	Part of an organ pipe which should be open and part of a preacher which should be closed.

Movable Doh	Cheque.
Movement	Part of a symphony or concerto. Different types of movement include fidgeting, coughing, dropping programme, and looking round the audience.
Music	Sound as organised by a composer to be misinterpreted by the conductor, not followed by the players and ignored by the audience.
Music examination	Test in irrelevant and archaic subjects, so designed to ensure that music qualifications are restricted to academics rather than musicians. If music colleges were responsible for the driving test, you would get a driving licence by knowing the history of the cartwheel.
Music graduate	Someone who believes that the world owes him a living and has yet to discover that the world does not share that opinion.
Music group	At least the second word is correct.
Music lesson	Punishment inflicted on children by their parents and on musicians by the demands of the tax authorities.
Music researcher	Person who has given up all hope of a love life.

Music stand   Device designed to cause the music to fall to the floor at the appropriate moment. Music stands come in two sizes: too high and too low. Students use music stands to make models of a pterodactyl skeleton.

Musica reservata   Performing *Carmina Burana* with some of the translation omitted.

Musical Joke   (1) Work by Mozart.
(2) Church music group

Musicians Union   Where mafia members go when expelled for bad behaviour.

Musicologist   Someone who finds the theory of music too exciting.

Musique concrete   Literally "concrete music". The term applies to the electronic organisation of sound to create a work. It is an area where the organist and music group may happily co-operate. The organist should be set in the musique …

Mutation   (1) Stop on an organ which plays harmonics.
(2) Person who sings in the treble section

Mute   What jazz trumpeters use and what you wish jazz trombonists were.

Mystery Convenient explanation for any theology believed without any basis.

Nail fiddle A good idea.

Naked fifth (1) Chord comprising just the tonic or dominant, without the mediant. (2) The soprano soloist who got the job.

Name tags Means by which choir members identify their robes, music, pigeon holes etc. By tradition, the names are of long-departed members of the choir. So a member says "I'll borrow Joe's music" when Joe is a bass who died in 1958.

Natural Term which means neither sharp nor flat, as in "the soprano appeared in her natural state to get to sing a solo."

Neapolitan Sixth Someone who loves ice cream.

Neck Where a guitar is hung and where the guitarist should be.

Nelson A mass by Haydn. An edited performance is known as a Half Nelson.

Netto (1) Italian term meaning "clear and distinct" (2) Used to catch a fisho.

New form of worship Another attempt to disband the choir.

New Wave Form of punk music enjoyed by organists when the music group is bathing in the sea.

Nine o'clock Traditional time for which a band is booked to play after a dinner and speeches. Nine o'clock British Gig Time approximates to half past ten Greenwich Mean Time.

Ninth Musical term for one over the eight.

Node Point of vibration in a string where C is immediately followed by F.

Noel Chap who turns up with Carol every Christmas.

None (1) Afternoon office of the Canonical Hours.
(2) Number of people who attend this service.

Nonet A musical work for nine people who can't go fishing.

Normal Term sometimes used to describe the keys of C major and A minor, and rarely used to describe an organist.

Notes

The basic unit of music. Organists like having lots of notes, particularly those from the Bank of England.

Notices

The ad lib part of a service designed to maintain its boredom factor. Some churches have notice sheets. These are full of details of bible passages the congregation doesn't read, names of the sick they don't pray for, bits of the service and so much other material that there is no room for the notices which are still given out verbally.

Nowell

Song sung at Christmas about having no water.

Nut

(1) Ridge over which the strings pass on a violin.
(2) Someone who plays one.

Nuts

Nutritious source of protein. Organists often commend them to lay readers.

Obelisk

Dagger-like sign in *Parish Psalter* to indicate a verse of a psalm that you cannot sing however many RSCM courses you have attended.

Oboe

Woodwind player who 'as no 'ouse.

Octave

Interval covered by 8 notes of a

scale, 12 semitones or 149 notes of a violin cadenza.

Octave coupler
Non-speaking stop used when the organist can still hear the vicar during a hymn.

Ode
What the trumpeter's rent is.

Off
(1) Direction to organist to remove a stop or coupler.
(2) Direction from an organist to church member who criticises the music, usually preceded by an Anglo-Saxon verb.

Offenbach
What dogs often do.

Offertory
Part of the service where the collection is taken. The organist may be required to play suitable music. This should be quiet enough for everyone to hear when copper coins are put in the bag.

Oil drum
(1) Instrument played by Caribbean musicians.
(2) What an Irishman says when he wants to join a band.

Oliphant
Large creature with a trunk and tusks.

Omniscience
The state of knowing everything. Only God is truly omniscient, though organists can come close.

Open Synod Group of members of General Synod which you join if you don't believe in joining groups.

Opera Performance in which long music is relieved by watching fat people in velvet clothes walk among pieces of hardboard, singing in a foreign language.

Opera buffa Stage work where the costumes have not arrived.

Opera house Organisation set up to raise funds for velvet clothes, hardboard scenery and singers who can sing in a foreign language while walking.

Opera plot There are two: boy gets girl, and boy does not get girl.

Opera seria Opera comique that is not supposed to be.

Operetta South African telephonist.

Optimist Professional musician with a mortgage.

Opus Work which describes a beautiful cat.

Orchestra Group of people in similar colour clothing and armed with various implements to confront another group of people, but who are not riot police.

Ordination   Process by which clergy wrongly believe they become invested with all human wisdom. In fact, this is not achieved by ordination but by learning to play the organ.

Organ   King of instruments. The organ is only mastered by those with supreme intelligence, unparalleled co-ordination, unsurpassable skill, incomparable expertise, ravishing good looks and unquestioned modesty. The organist is the source of all wisdom and the fount of all knowledge. It is for this reason that the organist must be recognised as the final authority on all matters musical and religious. His decision must not be questioned by those holding lower ranks, such as vicar. The organist must be treated with the utmost respect as a superior being who graciously deigns to honour the church with his presence.

Organ key   It is a time-honoured tradition that the key to the organ should be in a place which is far from obvious and that no-one who knows where it is should be at church when a visiting organist is playing.

Organ practice	Private performance of a duet for organ and vacuum cleaner.
Organ scholar	The usual excuse for not paying the deputy organist.
Organ student	Someone who is allowed to gain valuable experience by playing the organ at services the paid organist does not want to do.
Organist	Someone who plays the organ in church or finds someone else to play it in a cathedral.
Organo pleno	Instruction to drown the choir.
Organum	Term which has had no meaning since the 12th century and is therefore widely included in music exams.
Ornaments	Marks which indicate that Bach does not want you to play what he wrote but something much more complicated which does not fit.
Ossia	An alternative to the music written. Believed to be named after Ossies, who would rather go to the pub than play music at all.
Ostinato	Mood of the organist on a good day.
Overblowing	Practice of producing extra notes,

as used by woodwind players and
agents of soprano soloists.

Overstrung   Term used to describe either a piano
or a concert pianist.

Ox Minuet   Work wrongly attributed to Haydn,
though it doesn't really matter as
oxen don't dance much anyway.

Oxford Movement   Group which established itself in
the second half of the 19th century
with the aim of filling churches
with expensive clutter to stop
future generations doing what they
wanted.

Oxymoron   Term which contradicts itself, such
as "bittersweet", "clerical wisdom",
"brilliant guitarist", "modest
organist" and "Microsoft Works".

P   Instruction for musicians to play at
any volume they like. It is believed
to be an abbreviation for "pretty
loud".

Page turn   Point in the score where publishers
arrange to print difficult passages,
such as unexpected key changes.

Palindrome   Something which sounds the same
when played backwards, like most
modern music.

Pan

Primitive wind instrument on which it is difficult to get a tune. The alternative is to put it with some kettledrums and cook dinner.

Papal infallibility

Belief that the Pope cannot be wrong when making official pronouncements. Protestants believe that this doctrine is the clearest evidence that this is not so.

Parallel fifths

(1) When two organists are drinking Jack Daniels.
(2) Poor harmony writing, possibly after drinking too many Jack Daniels.

Parallel motion

The organist getting off the bench as the music group leader picks up his guitar.

Pardon?

The standard answer when someone asks you why you play the organ so loudly.

Parental responsibility Good idea.

Part song

Song written for different voices. So-called because you only get partway through before the altos need their note again.

Passing note

What the organist does to the choir when he has run out of Mint Imperials.

Passion   Oratorio traditionally performed
                             before Easter. For many musicians
                             this is the only passion in their
                             lives.

Pathetic   Tchaikovsky's sixth symphony,
                             which evokes the choir's attempts
                             to sing Tudor music.

Patience   A virtue admired in the driver
                             behind you and resented in the
                             driver in front.

Pause   What the choir should put on the
                             last note, and what the choirmaster
                             should not put on the sopranos.

Pavan   Large vehicle used to transport
                             amplification equipment.

Peace   Part of a Communion service where
                             members of the congregation shake
                             hands and pretend they like each
                             other, hence the expression "taking
                             the peace".

Pedals   Device to allow organists to play
                             wrong notes with their feet as well
                             as their hands.

Peg   Lady who tunes stringed
                             instruments.

Penny whistle   An old simple wind instrument.
                             No-one knows exactly how old they

are, except that they now cost at least two pounds.

Pentatonic   Requiring five gins.

Percussion   Things which a musician is required to hit. They include drums, cymbals, gongs, bells, woodblocks, guitars, curates, lay readers, music group, worship committee, and congregation members who moan about the anthem.

Perfect cadence   Two chords which conclude a soprano cadenza.

Perfect pitch   When you throw the music group's guitar into the skip and it lands exactly on top of their drums.

Perpetual canon   Someone who has been at the cathedral even longer than the head verger.

Perpetual curate   A clergyman who retains a low position during his working life. Such a clergyman has no delusions of grandeur, and is therefore now rarely found in the Church of England.

Pesante   (1) Heavy, like a mallet.
(2) Member of congregation who does not like the music and should be dealt with by a mallet.

Philistines

Barbarous people who occupied much of the Palestinian plain in Old Testament times. They were noted for lacking appreciation of music and fine art. They were defeated by Kings Jonathan and David, but regained their power. They are now found at theological colleges and in worship committees.

Photographer

Person who conducts a wedding in the Church of England.

Photographs

It is a church tradition that a choir vestry has photographs of the choir. Under canon law there must be no photograph less than 20 years old, and only one less than 40 years old.

Phrase

What happens to a cassock on a stone floor.

Phrasing

This is an important aspect of singing, as in the hymn
My God I love thee not; because I hope for heaven thereby.

Phyrgian

Term which either describes an ecclesiastical mode starting on E or the temperature of a choir vestry in winter.

Pianissimo

Indication that the band is ready for more drinks.

Piano	Piece of furniture for supporting beer glasses.
Piano cover	Large heavy piece of stitched cloth put over a piano in the hope that the music group will decide it is not worth the effort of taking it off and putting it back again.
Piano tuner	Someone who puts a piano out of tune so that he can put it back in tune again.
Picardy	Practice of ending a baroque work in a minor key with a major chord. The term is believed to be a mishearing when Bach was asked by a student "what shall I use as the mediant in this piece in B flat minor?"
Piccolo note	What second basses do.
Pick	What guitarists do with strings and what drummers do with their noses.
Pipe	Tube with holes in it. Small pipes are called flutes. Large pipes are called water mains.
Pirates of Penzance	How much Penn's mother's sisters charge for steak and kidney.
Piston	What the organist uses while thinking of what stops to use.

Piston Broke What a professional musician usually is.

Pitch (1) Determination of the frequency of a musical note and therefore where it appears on the scale and in which octave.
(2) A black substance useful for improving the vocal tone of the music group leader.

Pitch pipe (1) Device to give a note for tuning an instrument.
(2) What you want to do to the clarinet in the music group who does not use one.

Pits What theatre orchestras play in and what church music groups should play in.

Pizzicato tremolando Style of playing after having had too many drinks.

Plague Collective noun for worship group leaders.

Poco Italian for a little, based on what the conductor did and how the soprano soloist responded.

Pointing How to embarrass choristers who can't get the chant right.

Polyphony Parrot on the telephone.

Polytonality	Simultaneous use of two or more keys. The colloquial term is a damn awful row.
Pomposo	In the style of a theological college principal.
Ponderous	When a clergyman takes a long time to work out something daft to say.
Positif	Choir organ, from the expression "are you sure that was the right note?"
Positive organ	Part of the organ which provides clear and bright happy sounds. The negative organ is the mouth of the vicar's wife.
Posaune	Term used by builders of electronic organs to indicate the sound of a bee in a jam jar.
Post horn	(1) Long straight brass musical instrument. (2) What you do when the horn player is not looking.
Posthumous	Work written by a composer after he dies, not to be confused with decomposing.
Postlude	Sending Playboy by mail.
Practice	Last resort of an organist about to give a recital.

Precentor

Person in charge of singing in a cathedral. One who appears on *Songs of Praise* is called a television precentor.

Prelude

The easy bit Bach wrote to trick you into playing one of his fugues.

Preparatory beat

What a choirmaster threatens the choir with.

Prick-song

Term used between the 15th and 18th centuries for a song which is written down and not improvised. We can think of other definitions.

Primate

(1) An archbishop.
(2) A monkey.

Procession

Opportunity for the congregation to see the guilty parties.

Prodigy

Musician who can perform at a younger than normal age. A prodigy is typically someone who can sing at the age of two, play an instrument at six, compose a tune at seven, put up a music stand at 15 or play the guitar properly at 25.

Professional musician Someone who, when asked if he can play on 14 September, asks "how much?" rather than "what music is it?"
Other hallmarks of a professional

musician are knowing how to put up a music stand, having a roll of Gaffer tape with him, and moaning about how much he is being paid.

Programme

Booklet provided at concerts telling you what should have been performed and who should have been performing it, accompanied by brief notes about the music and detailed notes about the performers.

Progression

(1) Movement of two or more chords in succession
(2) When the music group leader is allowed to make coffee.

Prose

Professional musicians.

Psalm 23

The lyrics for the *Vicar of Dibley* theme.

Psalm 169

Indication on a service sheet that the church secretary does not fully understand the subtleties of church music.

Public address

Amplification system. Its function is to produce hisses and crackles so that you cannot hear what is being said.

Pulpit

Where the sermon is delivered. It is a contraction of the words "pulp it" which describes the value of most preaching.

Purcell　　　　　　　Old spelling of a washing powder.

Quarter note　　　　(1) How Americans describe a crotchet.
(2) Reminder that the trumpeter cannot pay the rent.

Quarter tone　　　　Interval of half a semitone. They are known to ancient Greeks, modern composers and guitar tuners.

Quavers　　　　　　Notes named after a popular snack.

Quickstep　　　　　When the organist hears that the vicar is looking for him.

Quint　　　　　　　Stop to help organists play discords.

Quitter　　　　　　(1) French term describing how to play a stringed instrument.
(2) English term describing an organist at an evangelical church.

Rackett　　　　　　Old reed instrument and the sound it made.

Ragtime　　　　　　When a trumpeter is told to wear evening dress.

Rain　　　　　　　Rain damages most musical instruments, so only the music group should be asked to play for outdoor services.

Random number　　How much a soprano soloist says she is worth.

Rank

(1) Collection of pipes in an organ.
(2) Collection of musicians in a worship group.

Rant

Old English dance, still occasionally performed in some churches.

Rataplan

Paying Rentokil in instalments.

Rattle

Percussion instrument often found in organists' cars.

Reading

A spoken part of a service, inexplicably named after a rock festival.

Real presence

Something better than a diary or cuff-links.

Realization

(1) Modern practice of following implicit instructions in a musical work to bring out its true meaning.
(2) Process of becoming aware that no-one cares a fig about your efforts at (1).

Recapitulation

Part of a sonata denoting when the vicar gave in to the organist again.

Recessional

Piece of music played after a service where the church has outlined its financial plans.

Recitative

Bits of an oratorio which are sung by a single person over a simple accompaniment to move the story along. Without recitatives, the whole story would have to be told in arias which would mean that an Easter Passion would finish around the middle of August.

Recorder	Instrument played by a judge.
Reed	Something a music group leader cannot do. He can't spell either.
Reeds	Things which naturally belongs in a swamp, like saxophones.
Refrain	Not singing the chorus.
Regal	Either a type of organ or a type of organist.
Rehearsal	The action of desperate musicians.
Rehearsal mark	Found on the body of someone who can't play the music properly.
Relative minor	A trumpet player's girlfriend.
Relish	Ornament put on food.
Repeat	When musicians use a phrase which has already been heard, such as "what are you drinking?"
Repercussion	(1) Reappearance of a fugue subject after the exposition.

	(2) Consequences of playing it when the vicar is trying to say a prayer.
Reproaches	(1) Anthems and responses sung on Good Friday. (2) Instructions to choir for the rest of the year.
Responses	Part of the service where the choir responds to what the minister has said. Common responses include "and also with you", "and make thy chosen people joyful" and "you must be joking".
Rest	(1) Silent bars in music. (2) What a musician cannot do while counting them.
Resting	Unemployment (particularly in the acting profession).
Retreat	What clergy go on to advance the cause of Christianity —which explains a lot.
Rheinberger	German take-away.
Rhythm	Method practised by certain members of a band in the hope of not producing any more.
Richard Strauss	Member of the Strauss family who was not related to any of the others.

Ring   Symbol of marriage. The three common rings are engagement ring, wedding ring and suffer ring.

Risoluto   Indication to maintain the current tempo regardless of what the conductor is indicating.

Ritard   Musical term for a church music group leader.

Ritenuto   Getting tired.

Robes   Plain garments worn over ordinary clothes to show that we are all equal before God. Organists and choristers often also wear hoods and medals to show how high up they are in this equality.

Roll   Sound from rapid beats on a drum. The various forms include a paid performance known as a bread roll; a theatrical performance called a ham roll; an improvised performance known as a jam roll; and a silly performance known as a sausage roll.

Rolling Stones   Popular group that gathered no moss, which may explain why they're still getting no satisfaction in their 60s.

Romance   Form of music rarely performed by organists.

Rood screen	Piece of architecture across the chancel. The choir sits behind it to make rood gestures.
Rosin	Question asked by Rosalind's boyfriend.
Rostrum	Raised platform which a conductor stands on so that the musicians find it easier to see the person they are ignoring.
Round	(1) Form of music where the voices come in one after the other. (2) Number of drinks which assist such performance.
Rubato	Indication that music may be performed in a free style as the performer wishes. This term is not necessary on parts for violas or solo sopranos.
Runs	Long passages, and why you need to go down them in a curry house.
Rural dean	Clergyman with oversight of clergy in a deanery. He is so-called because he is neither rural nor a dean.
SATB	Sack All The Basses.
Sackbut	What happens when Butt plays drinking songs after the sermon.

Sax shop
Place visited by a musician with a hearing impediment.

Saxophone
The funniest joke known to a clarinettist.

Scale
A series of notes in a predetermined order. It also refers to the other popular way of getting out of prison.

Scheidt
German composer (1587-1654). His name is pronounced "shite". He wrote many organ accompaniments and transcriptions. Many organists wrongly attribute worship songs to him.

Schlag
German term for either a beat or the drummer's girlfriend.

Score
(1) Music copy showing what should be played.
(2) Number of beers drunk before this is managed.

Scoring
Either writing out parts for an orchestra or what you would rather be doing.

Scotch snap
(1) Syncopation played in reverse order.
(2) What caused the syncopation to be played that way.

Scotch symphony   Mendelssohn's third symphony, at least half of which is loved by musicians everywhere.

Scratch band   A band put together for one concert, or a string orchestra put together for many.

Sea Drift   Song orchestrated by Delius, and how the baritone solo is likely to sing it.

Second half   Indication in a psalter that you are playing the wrong bit of the chant.

Second inversion   (1) Chord whose bottom note is the dominant.
(2) How to deal with a choirboy who obtained more sweets.

Second violinist   The most honest member of the orchestra.

Secular music   Music which is devoid of any religious influence, such as that used at family services.

Secularism   The process of removing God from every aspect of human life, and then asking where God is when something goes wrong.

Semi-chorus   Choir when there is a good programme on TV.

Senza	Musical term which means "without", as in *senza bass guitar, senza drums, senza worship group.*
Senza sordino	A term used to remind a brass player that he forgot to put his mute in a few bars back.
Septave	Term used by organ builders who cannot count up to eight.
Serial music	Examples include Coco-pops, Hornflakes and Weetabax.
Serious musician	One who plays with his eyes shut. Normally to be avoided.
Sermon	Part of the service where the organist sorts out his voluntary and the choir have a chance to catch up on their sleep. A sermon at the carol service indicates that the minister is trying to sack the organist, disband the choir and empty the church.
Service	Something the church provides and call centres don't.
Sesquialtera	Organ mixture stop of two ranks provided by an organ builder who is bored with using the word "mixture".
Sevenfold amen	Device to make very sure that there are no more prayers.

Sextet Six people who know each other very well.

Shagbut Alternative name for a sackbut, but which seems to have dropped from polite use for some reason.

Shake An old musical ornament. The others are known as the Rattle and Roll.

Shakes Effect in music produced either by a rapid alternation of notes or by asking the organist to play *If I Were a Butterfly.*

Share How an evangelical says "tell". So "I would like to share with you" means that the speaker is about to say something highly offensive, personal and completely daft.

Sharp Symbol used for playing noughts and crosses, and how you must look when the choirmaster catches you doing so.

Shepherds pipe Old rustic instrument, often sold to hungry workers who don't speak properly.

Shift Changing from one position to another. In music, examples include violinists and trombonists using another position, a keyboard player moving his left hand, and the organist putting the music group instruments out in the rain.

Shoe polish   Something which organists should use, according to soprano soloists who say it tastes nice.

Shofar   Sho' good.

Silk   (1) Type of worm
(2) Senior barrister

Singer   Musician who is too mean to buy an instrument and too lazy to learn how to play it. Singers have long been held in contempt. Even Jesus was criticised for mixing with singers and tax-gatherers.

Sleigh bells   Instrument added to a pop song issued before Christmas.

Slur   Indication that the music is to be played the way the organist speaks.

Soloist   The person who the musicians have previously agreed will take the blame for a bad performance.

Solti   Hungarian conductor (1912-1997). He has a type of potato crisp named after him.

Songs of Fellowship Books which fills up a space in church where the hymn books once were.

Soprano Female singer who can impersonate strangled cats and nails being scraped down a blackboard.

Sotto voce Musical term for how comments on the sermon should be made when the preacher is in earshot.

Sound What music is and the sermon is not.

Sound quality Something of great concern to sound engineers and of no concern to church music groups.

Soundboard How children respond to the preacher's questions at a family service.

Space What lies between two lines of a musical stave or between the ears of a music group leader.

Spatial music Music where the position of the performers is considered important to the quality of performance. For example, a performance by the worship group may be improved by having the singers in a room next door, the guitarist in the car park and the drummer six feet under the car park.

Speaking in tongues Saying things in a language which no-one understands. This is regarded as a gift of the Holy Spirit in the charismatic church, and as normal preaching in most other denominations.

Speed of sound This is about 772 miles per hour, showing that however keen you are to get away from the sound, it is even keener to get away from you.

Spinet Keyboard instrument similar to harpsichord. Care must be taken when moving one within the hearing of a preacher as "spinet out" could be misinterpreted.

Spiral staircase Part of organ console designed to discourage anyone from using the rest of it.

Spirit-filled Either a Christian from the charismatic movement or an organist about one hour after the end of choir practice.

Spit valve How horn players express their opinion of the music.

Spirituality Belief in God but without either belief or God.

Spoonerism When the diocese of St Albans prays for "our dear queen".

Stained glass

(1) Decorative windows in a traditional church.
(2) What happens when no-one does the washing up after a choir party.

Stainer's Crucifixion

Good idea.

Steel drums

Another good idea.

Stigma

Sign of suffering born by the mother of the chap who test-drives cars on *Top Gear*.

Stockhausen

Most councils now have laws which require dog owners to remove this from the pavements.

Stole

Part of clerical dress. A priest should wear it straight down, a deacon diagonally and a worship group leader tightly round the neck.

Stop

Means by which an organ produces music and a music group improves the quality of its music.

Stops

Devices on pipe organs which produce different tones, and which on electronic organs all produce the same tone.

Strain

Part of a tune produced by working with the music group.

Streng

(1) German for "severe".
(2) Chelsea-speak for "string"

Strings	Conditions you must accept to get enough violins.
Stück	(1) German term for "piece" (2) English term for tenors describing their sight-reading.
String quartet	A Soviet symphony orchestra after touring the USA.
String quintet	Local branch of the piano haters society.
Style	Term which describes the character of a piece of music, and does not describe the organist's appearance.
Sub dean	Naval chaplain.
Subdominant	The fourth note of a scale. (The term sounds like something much more exciting, but writers of music harmony books have never been very good on sex appeal.)
Subito piano	Indication that an obscure member of the orchestra is playing a solo.
Submission	Meekly surrendering, as when a worship leader yields to the will of God. Not as good as a knock-out.
Suite	Series of musical items which convey a single idea. A dreamy idea is called a bedroom suite; one

comprising three sections is known as a three-piece suite; one that is difficult to play is called a sticky suite; and one that has a hot feel is known as a boiled suite.

Sunrise service   Service held at an indecently early hour on Easter Day to punish organists who were out gigging the previous night.

Supertonic   What is needed with a good gin.

Suspended fourth   When the organist is having a good day dealing with the music group.

Suspension   Device which either introduces temporary dissonance in harmony or introduces permanent harmony in a music group.

Sustaining pedal   Device on a piano used when the music gets too difficult.

Sweet wrappers   Material used to keep cassock pockets in shape.

Swell   (1) Organ which is enclosed in a box.
(2) Tenor soloist who should be enclosed in a box.

Swell box   (1) Device for regulating the volume on the upper manual on an organ.
(2) Large number of chocolates.

Swing

Form of jazz which became popular in the 1930s. Music groups should be encouraged to swing. The organist may care to donate the rope.

Sympathetic strings

Found on sitars and clavichords. Not found in orchestras.

Syncopation

Moving uneasily from bar to bar. Also known as a pub crawl.

Taizé chant

Indication that the organist needs to bring a hip flask and a good book to the service.

Takt

(1) German term for "measure"
(2) English term for what the organist needs.

Talon

The heel of a violin bow or the fingernail of a soprano who was not asked to sing a solo.

Tam tam

Gong played by two Scotsmen.

Tambourine

Something which is full of jingles, has a large amount of skin, is often bashed, but is not Channel 5 television.

Tangent

Part of a harpsichord mechanism employed by vicar when the organist wishes to discuss music.

Tango

Lively dance by orange people with lots of fizz who want to get canned.

Tape recorder

Lie detector used against singers.

Tarantella

Large Italian spider.

Te Deum

Very long canticle. The term is believed to be a Latin form for "tedious".

Temperament

(1) System of tuning instruments. (2) State of the person after trying to do so.

Tempo

Speed at which music is performed. This is traditionally about a third slower than at rehearsals with the violas half a beat behind.

Tempo giusto

Indication that it is about time the musician played at the right speed.

Ten

Musical term which either means "hold" or indicates how many the organist thinks he can.

Tenor

The choral equivalent of the dodo.

Tenth

Adding a third to an eighth, proving that music is not a branch of mathematics.

The Ring

Cycle of four operas written by Wagner. It has three rates of admission: under 16, over 16, and those who become 16 during the performance.

The Vicar Writes Something which sometimes appears in a parish magazine. Some parishes have vicars that can read as well.

Theologian The man on the beach busily digging a hole to find the sunshine.

Theological query American ordinand.

Theology The only subject where the more you study, the less you know.

Theology lecturer Someone who talks in someone else's sleep.

Thirteenth Polite name for a discord in jazz. If accompanied with any further comments such as "sus 4" or "b 5", it is sufficient that the pianist sits on the keyboard.

Thirty-second symphony As composed by Mozart and Haydn. It is surprising that four movements can be fitted into thirty seconds.

Thorough-bass Member of the choir who stays behind to look for his missing cough sweets.

Throat infection   Indication that a soprano soloist
does not feel properly valued on
the day before a performance.
Temporary relief may be found
from sipping simple linctus.
Permanent relief comes from saying
"don't worry, I know another young
keen soprano who will welcome
this chance to advance her career.
You just rest tomorrow; I'll give her
a call."

Tie   Something often seen over the notes
in choral music and rarely seen
round the neck of an organist.

Time   Something counted by players and
served by choirmasters.

Time for reflection   Something clergy say they need
when they are not getting their own
way.

Toccata   Piece of organ music written by
Bach or Widor.

Toilet   Feature in church buildings
from about 1950 before which
churchgoers apparently had
completely different bodily
functions. The number of toilets is
calculated according to the formula
$n = (t - 4) \div 3$, where n is the
number of toilets provided and t is
the number of toilets needed.

Tom tom	Drum played by two Irishmen.
Tombola	Popular item at a church fete. Typically people pay £1 for a 1 in 5 chance of winning an item worth 75p which they donate to the next fete as a tombola prize. Some tie presses and toilet roll covers are believed to have been won more than 30 times.
Tone	Musical term which indicates either the quality of musical sound or that Tony should play the solo.
Tone deafness	Occupational hazard for choir members. Job requirement for music group leaders.
Tone row	The 12 chromatic notes of an octave in a predetermined sequence as used in the compositions of Schoenberg. Those who like this music pronounce the second word to rhyme with "go".
Tonic	The key note in a piece of music, and what a tenor puts in his gin to celebrate finally finding it.
Tonic sol-fa	Padded chair to sit on and drink gin.
Total immersion	Traditional form of baptism where a person is put completely under

the surface of water for a second or so, unless the person is a member of the music group when they should be baptised for at least ten minutes as a tribute to their musical spirituality.

Tradition   The church rule that if you have done something wrong for long enough you must keep on doing it.

Traditional   A composer who lived between 1200 and 1960 in many different countries at the same time and wrote much simple though beautiful music.

Transposing instrument

Woodwind instrument which is designed to play notes at the wrong pitch. The composer is obliged to write these parts in a different key, thus helping to ensure that they get their fair quota of wrong notes.

Transposition   Changing the key from being too low for the basses to being too high for the sopranos.

Treble   Child who sings the top line, so called because it takes three attempts to get anything right.

Tremulant   Device on an organ to make it sound like the sopranos.

Triangle	Small percussion instrument which reminds orchestra players why their love lives are in a mess.
Trinity	A subject of no interest to anyone except preachers, who then tell us that it is too difficult to preach about.
Trio	Term meaning three and which is therefore used as a middle section for any number of players. An exception is a trio sonata in four parts.
Triple time	Rate for playing at a wedding on Christmas Eve.
Tritus	The third of the authentic modes, starting on F. The opposite is *detritus,* which mode is often used for worship songs.
Trombone	Fog horn fitted with a slide.
Trombone stop	Good idea.
Trot	Political viewpoint of a musician who has yet to earn any money.
Trout Quintet	Five experienced sopranos singing Schubert.
Trumpet	Stop on an organ, so named because it sounds nothing like a trumpet.

Tuba Air raid siren controlled by an organist.

Tutti Indication that all musicians want some frutti.

Tutu Ballerina's frilly skirt worn by university graduates who did not get a first.

Tuxedo Black dinner jacket which comes in two sizes: too small and too big.

Typing errors Proof that word processors can be demonically possessed comes from service sheets which say:
I know that my Redeemer lies
Her would I touch and handle things unseen
All around Thy throne, a thong....
Snug mattins; Evensnog

Ukulele Instrument which few people can either play properly or spell properly.

Unaccompanied When a choir sings without the organ playing. For some reason, this often makes the organ suddenly go sharp.

Unessential notes Worship songs.

Unicorns Two animals which criticised Noah's taste in music.

Unison	The trade union which protests that the choir does not have enough four-part music to sing.
United Reformed	Anglicanism done badly.
Upright piano	One which has never been to the pub or used for rugby songs.
Variations	Work in which a composer includes all his early ideas.
Verse	Section of a song. One which talks of love is called Con Verse; one which promotes something is called Ad Verse; one which praises the music group is called Per Verse.
Vestry	Place where the church keeps old robes, broken coat hangers, old service sheets and boxes of indeterminate items left over from the last fete.
Vibrato	A device used by singers to hide the fact that they are on the wrong note.
Vicar	Person to whom the organist delegates the routine business of running a church.
Viol	Something which describes a predecessor to the violin and how it sounded.

Violin family	Troubled family known to social services. Violin is highly strung and complains a lot. Her sister Viola suffers from a persecution complex. Cello has difficulties getting on with others. Double Bass tends to be a loner who mumbles to himself.
Violins	Instruments where you need a lot of them to sound good — a fact organists should repeatedly mention.
Virginal	Description used for harpsichords rather than soprano soloists.
Virtuoso	Singer who is almost as good as she thinks she is.
Vision	Unrealistic idea from a bored vicar.
Visitation	When a bishop or other senior churchman makes a formal visit to a church. The parish typically makes great efforts to tidy up, the congregation are press-ganged into attending, great care is taken in the production of the service and service sheets, and the organist arranges special music with imported musicians. This allows the bishop to form a favourable opinion of what an ordinary service is like there.

Vocal range   The series of notes which a person can comfortably sing. A trained singer has a range of about two octaves, an untrained singer of one and half octaves, and a dance band singer of about five notes.

Vocals   Term used in popular music as an admission that a person cannot actually sing.

Voluntary   Piece of music played by an organist in a service, particularly at the end.
In churches with inspired leadership, good preaching and deep spiritual values, the voluntary is valued as fine music with which to conclude worship.
In churches with poor leadership, bad preaching and shallow spiritual values, the voluntary is tolerated as background noise while the congregation gets its coffee.

Wax   (1) Substance which melts in candles.
(2) What the sidesman gets when it drips on the carpet.

We Believe in God   Statement issued by the House of Bishops in the Church of England. The voting figures have never been disclosed.

Welcomer	Person who obstructs visitors to evangelical churches in a bid to stop them coming back.
Wind	(1) Unpleasant gas escaping from the body. (2) Collective term for flutes, oboes, clarinets, trumpets, horns etc
Wind machine	Someone who has eaten too many baked beans and liquorice allsorts.
Witchcraft	A broom usually.
Wolf	Term which describes a sound produced by either playing a note in the wrong temperament or when seeing a young girl in a mini-skirt.
Working party	Group set up by a vicar to agree with him and to share the blame when the idea is proved to be daft.
World premier	Last performance of a commissioned work.
Worship	Ego trip for the music group.
Worship committee	Forum for exchanging ignorance.
Worship leader	Someone who is wasting his talents as a supermarket shelf stacker.
Worship group	What a church uses after it has decided to discontinue having music in its services.

Xylophone solo   Indication that the work was written by an American composer.

Yawn   The only occasion a PCC member gets to open his mouth when the minister is speaking.

Yodel   Type of singing used to make cheese.

Young person   Anyone in church under the age of 40.

Youth leader   Person who may be used by the organist if wanting to see the reaction by someone with no appreciation of music. The organist should be kind to the youth leader, as he is probably the only person treated less well than the organist.

Youth service   Service intended for young people. The main characteristics of a youth service are:

(a) half of those who should be there don't turn up;

(b) those who do turn up look at each other in embarrassed silence as they don't know what to do next

(c) the music is chosen by the young people to reflect the spirituality of the service, ie they choose their favourites;

(d) the service is designed to attract young people;

(e) it doesn't;

(f) the vicar declares it a great success.

Zu   German for "to", and where choirboys should be sent to.